I've Got a Rock in My Pocket

HANNAH SOUTHARD

ISBN 978-1-0980-7186-8 (paperback)
ISBN 978-1-0980-7187-5 (digital)

Christian Faith Publishing, Inc.
832 Park Avenue
Meadville, PA 16335
www.christianfaithpublishing.com

Printed in the United States of America

I've got a rock in my pocket. I found it on an adventure. It is gray and shiny. I knew it looked special, so I picked it up to keep with me on my next adventure.

On an adventure to see Granny, something amazing happened.

"I've got a rock in my pocket," I told Granny. "Let me show you."

I pulled it out and let her look at it. Granny told me she knew a story about how God used a rock to give some people exactly what they needed when they needed it.

"After Moses led the Israelites out of Egypt, they were in the desert. The desert is very hot and dry. They had no water. They were begging God for water. So God told Moses to strike a rock, and water would come out. Moses did exactly as God told him, and water came out for all the people. Even in the most hopeless times, God will provide [Exodus 17:1–7]."

On an adventure to see Mossy and Grandpa, something remarkable happened.

"I've got a rock in my pocket," I told Mossy and Grandpa. "Let me show you."

I pulled it out and let them look at it. Mossy told me God gave us his special rules on a rock:

1. Do not worship any other gods.
2. Do not make any idols.
3. Do not misuse the name of God.
4. Keep the Sabbath holy.
5. Honor your father and mother.
6. Do not murder.
7. Do not commit adultery.
8. Do not steal.
9. Do not lie.
10. Do not covet.

On an adventure to see Jack, Luke, and Reed, something incredible happened.

"I've got a rock in my pocket," I told Jack, Luke, and Reed. "Let me show you."

I pulled it out and let them look at it. Jack told me he knew a story about how God helped a small guy use a tiny rock to defeat a big man.

"Goliath and the Philistines terrorized the Israelites. None of the Israelites were brave enough to stand up to them. David knew he couldn't defeat Goliath on his own, but God could through him. David got a small stone and a slingshot and defeated Goliath. Once the Philistines saw this, they ran away with fear. David gave God all the glory. So David won the fight against Goliath with a sling and a stone [1 Samuel 17:50])."

On an adventure to see Memaw and Papaw, something astounding happened.

"I've got a rock in my pocket," I told Memaw and Papaw. "Let me show you."

I pulled it out and let them look at it. Memaw told me she knew a memory verse about God being our rock.

"The Lord is my rock, my fortress, and my deliverer, my God, my rock where I seek refuge, my shield and the horn of my salvation, my stronghold [Psalm 18:2]."

On an adventure to see Lolli and Pops, something wonderful happened.

"I've got a rock in my pocket," I told Lolli and Pops. "Let me show you."

I pulled it out and let them look at it. Lolli told me she knew a song about building our life on God, who is our rock.

The wise man built his house upon the rock

The wise man built his house upon the rock

The wise man built his house upon the rock

And the rains came tumbling down

The rains came down and the floods came up

The rains came down and the floods came up

The rains came down and the floods came up

And the house on the rock stood firm

The foolish man built his house upon the sand

The foolish man built his house upon the sand

The foolish man built his house upon the sand

And the rains came tumbling down

The rains came down and the floods came up

The rains came down and the floods came up

The rains came down and the floods came up

And the house on the sand went smash
So build your life on the Lord Jesus Christ,
So build your life on the Lord Jesus Christ,
So build your life on the Lord Jesus Christ,
And the blessings will come down.
The blessings come down as your prayers go up,
The blessings come down as your prayers go up,
The blessings come down as your prayers go up,
So build your life on the Lord.
(Matthew 7:24–27)

On an adventure to see Aunt Sherri and Uncle Billy, something awesome happened.

"I've got a rock in my pocket," I told Aunt Sherri and Uncle Billy. "Let me show you."

I pulled it out and let them look at it. Aunt Sherri told me she knew a scripture about how even a rock knows who God is.

"I tell you, if they were to keep silent, the stones would cry out [Luke 19:40]."

Jesus was telling the people that even if we didn't tell people about Jesus, nature itself would have to because Jesus is worthy of all praise.

On an adventure to church, something marvelous happened.

"I've got a rock in my pocket," I told my Sunday school teacher, Mr. Bobby. "Let me show you."

I pulled it out and let him look at it. Mr. Bobby told me he knew a story about Jesus saving a lady from a bunch of rocks.

"There was a lady that some men brought to Jesus. They told Jesus that she had sinned and deserved to be stoned. They were trying to test Jesus to see what He would do. Jesus stood with the lady and said, 'Let any one of you who is without sin be the first to throw a stone at her.' Once Jesus said this, one by one, the men began to leave. When they had all left, Jesus then asked the woman where her accusers were. She told him no one was left. So Jesus told her to go and sin no more. No one is without sin, and yet Jesus can forgive us all [John 8:2-11]."

On an adventure to see Grandpa and Gram-Mel, something miraculous happened.

"I've got a rock in my pocket," I told Grandpa and Gram-Mel. "Let me show you."

I pulled it out and let them look at it. Grandpa told me he knew a story about a giant rock meant to keep Jesus in the grave.

"When Jesus was teaching the people to love God and love others, some of them did not understand Him. So they became angry with Jesus and hung Him on a cross. They did not know that this was really God's plan all along: for Jesus to die for our sins. Jesus's body was placed in a grave. Then some strong men put a big rock in front of the grave to try to keep Jesus inside. When His mother and friends came to the grave three days later, the great big rock was rolled away, and an angel was sitting on it! The angel said to the women, 'He is not here, He is risen!' This is good news! JESUS IS ALIVE! [Luke 19:28–24; 53]"

Now I can show all my friends the rock in my pocket and tell them of the adventures that we have been on.

About the Author

Hannah Southard is a former elementary teacher and current stay-at-home mom who has a passion for telling young children about Christ. She is an active member of her church, First Baptist Church of Pasadena. She lives in League City, Texas, with her husband, Drew, and her two boys Keith Andrew and Kyle.

CPSIA information can be obtained
at www.ICGtesting.com
Printed in the USA
LVHW072333050521
686549LV00031B/1522

9 781098 071868